PREDATOR VS. PREY



# WOLVES VS. MOOSE

## FOOD CHAIN FIGHTS

BEN HUBBARD

Lerner Publications ◆ Minneapolis

For Kimbo



Lerner Publications Company
An imprint of Lerner Publishing Group, Inc.
241 First Avenue North
Minneapolis, MN 55401 USA

For reading levels and more information, look up this title at www.lernerbooks.com.

Main body text set in Aptifer Sans LT Pro.
Typeface provided by Linotype AG.

**Designer:** Kim Morales
**Lerner team:** Martha Kranes

**Library of Congress Cataloging-in-Publication Data**

Names: Hubbard, Ben, 1973– author.
Title: Wolves vs. moose : food chain fights / Ben Hubbard.
Other titles: Wolves versus moose
Description: Minneapolis : Lerner Publications, [2025] | Series: Predator vs. prey | Includes bibliographical references and index. | Audience: Ages 8–11 | Audience: Grades 4–6 | Summary: "Wolves and moose face off in this thrilling book. Young readers learn key features about each animal such as how they hunt, their speed, and more. Discover if the predator or prey dominates the habitat"— Provided by publisher.
Identifiers: LCCN 2023043403 | ISBN 9798765626788 (library binding) | ISBN 9798765629413 (paperback) | ISBN 9798765636329 (epub)
Subjects: LCSH: Gray wolf—Juvenile literature. | Moose—Juvenile literature. | Predation (Biology)—Juvenile literature. | Food chains (Ecology)—Juvenile literature.
Classification: LCC QL737.C22 H78 2025 | DDC 599.773—dc23/eng/20231204

LC record available at https://lccn.loc.gov/2023043403

Manufactured in the United States of America
1-1010125-52009-2/20/2024

# TABLE OF CONTENTS

# CHAPTER 1
# LAKE ATTACK

**ON A CLOUDY FALL DAY, A MOOSE STEPS INTO THE SHALLOWS OF A LAKE.** It drops its head to drink. Suddenly, it stops. As it lifts its head, its ears prick up. It can hear something moving in the nearby forest. Danger is coming the moose's way.

A gray wolf steps silently from the forest. It walks into the water and swims toward the moose. Its mouth opens wide, ready to attack. The moose lunges at the wolf with its front hooves. The wolf jumps back but swims forward again.

The moose runs farther into the lake. The wolf is just behind. It bites down on the moose's back leg. The moose shakes the wolf. But it won't let go.

Will the wolf get its prey? Or will the moose escape? Who will win in this battle of life or death—predator or prey?

A moose protects her calf from wolves.

Gray wolves and moose live in the forests of North America, Europe, and Russia. The gray wolf is North America's most common wolf species. It lives in packs and hunts large, hoofed prey. It often kills deer, caribou, and moose. A wolf pack's territory stretches between 31 to 1,200 square miles (80 to 3,100 sq. km).

Moose are the biggest members of the deer family. They are famous for their large size, long legs, and huge antlers. Their antlers can grow to be about 6 feet (1.8 m) across. But moose are not hunters. They are herbivores—they eat plants. They mostly live in forests and are eaten by grizzly bears and wolves.

A moose eats plants while swimming.

## GRAY WOLF STATS

**WEIGHT:** 31 to 143 pounds (14 to 65 kg)

**LENGTH:** up to 6.6 feet (2 m)

**HEIGHT:** 2.6 feet (0.8 m) at the shoulder

**TOP SPEED:** 37 miles (60 km) per hour

## MOOSE STATS

**WEIGHT:** 440 to 1,600 pounds (200 to 726 kg)

**LENGTH:** 8 to 10 feet (2.4 to 3 m)

**HEIGHT:** 7 feet (2.1 m) at the shoulder

**TOP SPEED:** 35 miles (56 km) per hour

# CHAPTER 2
# GRAY WOLVES VS. MOOSE

**GRAY WOLVES AND MOOSE FACE OFF IN A HEAD-TO-HEAD BATTLE.** Each has special features to help them win. Let's learn more about their strengths and see who rules the habitat.

## SIZE

Gray wolves and moose are both large mammals. The wolf is the biggest wild member of the dog family. It can weigh up to 143 pounds (65 kg), which is as heavy as some human adults. It also has long legs and big paws for walking across snow.

Moose can reach 7 feet (2.1 m) in height. That's as tall as a professional basketball player! Moose also have long, thin legs. This helps them walk through water and snow. A moose's front legs are longer than its back legs. This helps it jump over boulders and logs.

## WHINING WOLVES

Wolves talk to one another with yelps, whines, growls, and howls. But they don't howl at the moon!

A wolf's tail is about 1.6 feet (0.5 m) long.

Gray wolves can sprint for a short time.

## SPEED

Gray wolves have strong legs and padded paws to quickly sneak up on prey. They can reach speeds of 37 miles (60 km) per hour. That's nearly as fast as a zebra. Usually, wolves walk 5 miles (8 km) an hour.

## ANTLER AMPLIFIERS

**Only male moose grow antlers. The antlers may help them hear better. This is because they bounce sound into their ears.**

Moose can run at 35 miles (56 km) per hour. That is fast for an animal weighing up to 1,600 pounds (726 kg)! Moose have hard hooves. Each hoof has four toes. This helps them walk on soft and slippery surfaces.

Moose's toes help them run through the snow.

## SENSES

Gray wolves have powerful senses. Their sense of smell is about a hundred times stronger than that of a human. This lets them sniff out moose. When tracking a moose, a wolf uses its ears to hear faint, high-pitched sounds. Its eyes can then pick up small movements, even in low light conditions.

A wolf lifts its head to smell.

### HERD SMELL

**Wolves can smell a herd of moose from about 1.7 miles (2.8 km) away.**

Moose have trouble seeing, but their strong senses of hearing and smell help them.

Moose use their sense of hearing and smell to protect themselves. Their long noses sniff out predators from about 2 miles (3.2 km) away. Moose also smell the markings left behind by other moose. Moose ears move in different directions. This helps them hear where predators are coming from. Moose with antlers have a better sense of hearing.

Gray wolves swim with their heads held high and use their tails to push forward.

## SWIMMING

Gray wolves are strong swimmers. Their webbed paws help them paddle through the water. They can swim up to 7.5 miles (12 km) without stopping.

## DIVING DEEP

**Moose can dive 20 feet (6.1 m) underwater to feed on plants. The moose's nose has flaps that close when it dives.**

Moose can swim only days after being born. They feed on plants in lakes and streams. Moose can hold their breath underwater for up to one minute. They can also swim for long distances. Moose can swim at 6 miles (9.7 km) per hour! But they can only swim this fast for about two hours.

A moose and her calf swim together.

## KEY WEAPONS

Gray wolves use their powerful jaws and sharp teeth to attack. A wolf's bite can break through flesh and bone. Its front fangs can grow to 2.5 inches (6.4 cm) long. The wolf uses these fangs to puncture skin and grip onto prey to kill it. Its middle incisor teeth are like knives. They cut meat away from the bone. Its back molar teeth crush and grind.

Gray wolves have forty-two teeth.

## COAT COLORS

**Gray wolves are many different colors. They can be brown, tan, red, black, and even white. These colors help wolves blend in.**

A moose does a front kick.

A moose's main weapon is its killer kick. Its hard hooves can break bones and crush skulls. A moose often rears up and stomps with its front legs. But it can also kick in other directions. Its backward kick can be even more deadly than its front kick. It can easily kill a large animal with its kick.

Wolves are more likely to get their prey if they hunt in packs than on their own.

## FINDING FOOD

Gray wolves hunt by ambushing or surprising their prey. Their soft paws help them quietly creep. Then they sprint to attack. Wolves often hunt in packs. They surround their prey before striking together. But a wolf can also take on large prey alone. Hunting on their own or with a pack, wolves chase their prey, tire them out, and then strike.

Moose are herbivores, so they do not hunt their food. Instead, they spend their lives walking and feeding on plants. An adult moose can eat 40 to 70 pounds (18 to 32 kg) of leaves, twigs, and other vegetation every day.

A moose feeds on a plant.

## DEWLAP

**Most moose have a piece of skin hanging from their throats. This is a dewlap. It might show a young male is ready to mate.**

A wolf bites down on prey.

## ATTACK AND DEFENSE STYLES

Gray wolves attack by rushing at prey. Once they reach their target, wolves bite down hard. They aim for the neck to kill their prey quickly. They might also attack an animal's behind or side. Often it takes several bites for wolves to kill their prey.

### FLAT AND FRIENDLY

**Wolves communicate using body language. To be friendly with one another, wolves wag their tails and flatten their ears. Aggressive wolves stand still. They raise their tails and keep their ears forward.**

A moose steps toward an attacking wolf.

Moose protect themselves with their powerful kicks. If predators dodge the kick, they must back away before attacking again. When a moose does kick its attacker, the other animal needs time to recover, allowing the moose to get away. Moose can navigate difficult terrain at high speeds. They can also swim for long distances. This helps them escape danger.

## WEAKNESSES

Gray wolves are at risk from about eighty diseases. They can catch diseases from sick prey they eat. One of the diseases, distemper, is fatal. Wolves are also threatened by humans. Humans hunt wolves. They also destroy wolf habitats by cutting down trees and building where wolves live.

With fewer trees, there are fewer places for wolves to live, hide, and find prey.

## LEAVING MOOSE MOTHERS

**Young moose leave their mothers after one year. Then they spend the rest of their lives alone, except during mating.**

Snails are common in forest habitats.

Moose are at risk from parasites. One harmful parasite is a brain worm. Moose catch brain worms from deer poop, slugs, and snails. A brain worm can cause a moose to become so weak it falls over. Then it dies.

# CHAPTER 3
# RULER OF THE FOREST

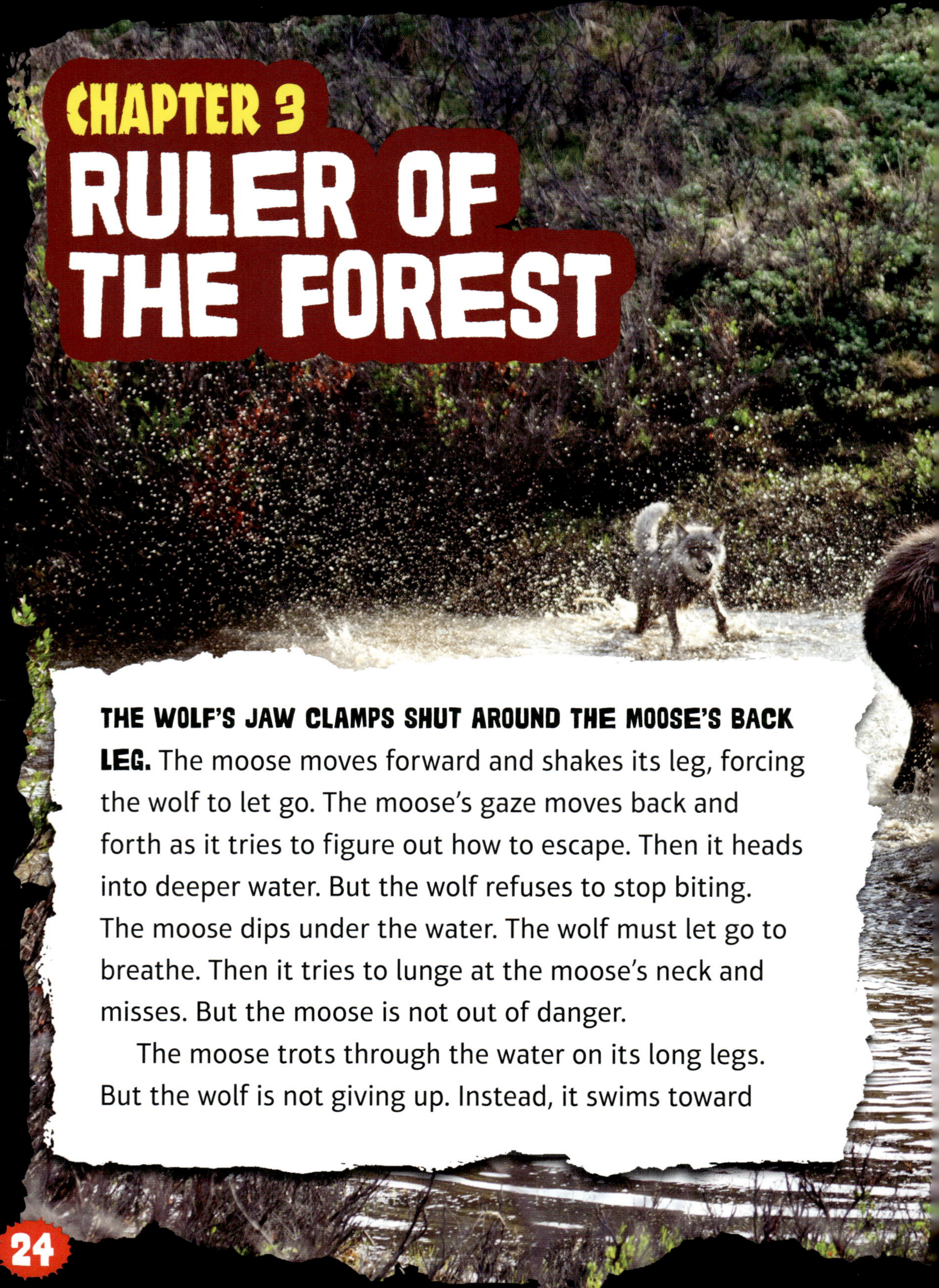

**THE WOLF'S JAW CLAMPS SHUT AROUND THE MOOSE'S BACK LEG.** The moose moves forward and shakes its leg, forcing the wolf to let go. The moose's gaze moves back and forth as it tries to figure out how to escape. Then it heads into deeper water. But the wolf refuses to stop biting. The moose dips under the water. The wolf must let go to breathe. Then it tries to lunge at the moose's neck and misses. But the moose is not out of danger.

The moose trots through the water on its long legs. But the wolf is not giving up. Instead, it swims toward

the moose. The moose swims even farther into the lake. The chase is on. But the distance between them keeps increasing. Finally, the wolf gives up and swims back to the edge of the lake. It shakes itself dry before walking into the forest. The moose has escaped death.

Wolves are fierce predators but don't always get their prey.

The gray wolf and moose are among the largest animals in their habitats. Gray wolves are one of the most successful predators in the world. They can easily kill large prey. A wolf often does this by chasing its prey until it is worn out.

Moose are also a highly successful species. Their kicks can kill an attacker. But they need to know how to escape. Moose can travel long distances at a fast speed. They don't tire easily. A moose can outrun a wolf. It faces a harder challenge if it is facing a wolf pack.

This time, the moose escaped. It was the stronger swimmer, going deeper and farther in the water than the wolf. After a while, the wolf had to give up. Tomorrow, things could be different. The wolf may attack and have help from its pack. Who knows what may happen? Nothing is certain in the battle between predators and prey.

The moose escaped the wolf's attack.

# PREDATOR VS. PREY: HEAD-TO-HEAD

## WOLF

- Big, padded paws for walking over snow
- Strong jaws and sharp teeth to tear through fur and flesh

## MOOSE

- Large antlers for fighting rival males
- Long, thin legs for walking though water

# GLOSSARY

**antlers:** the horns of a moose or similar animal

**habitat:** the place where a plant or animal naturally lives or grows

**hearing:** the sense through which a person or animal is aware of sound

**mammal:** a type of animal that feeds milk to its young and that usually has hair or fur covering most of its skin

**parasite:** a tiny creature that lives inside an animal and feeds off it

**predator:** an animal that hunts and kills other animals for food

**prey:** an animal that is hunted and killed for food by another animal

**sense:** the ways an animal understands its surroundings. Senses include touch, smell, taste, sight, and hearing.

**trot:** to move forward in a hurry

# LEARN MORE


Britannica Kids: Moose
https://kids.britannica.com/kids/article/moose/384796

Castaldo, Nancy F. *The Wolves and Moose of Isle Royale: Restoring an Island Ecosystem*. New York: Clarion Books, 2022.

Clasky, Leonard. *The Gray Wolf*. New York: Gareth Stevens, 2023.

Hubbard, Ben. *Lions vs. Zebras: Food Chain Fights*. Minneapolis: Lerner Publications, 2025.

*National Geographic Kids:* Gray Wolf
https://kids.nationalgeographic.com/animals/mammals/facts/gray-wolf

*National Geographic Kids:* Moose
https://kids.nationalgeographic.com/animals/mammals/facts/moose

# INDEX



# PHOTO ACKNOWLEDGMENTS

Image credits: Patrick J. Endres/Getty Images, pp. 4–5, 19, 21, 24–25; Scott Suriano/Getty Images, p. 6; KeithSzafranski/Getty Images, p. 7 (top); Chase Dekker Wild-Life Images/Getty Images, p. 7 (bottom); blickwinkel/Alamy, pp. 8–9; Joe McDonald/Getty Images, p. 10; franzfoto.com/Alamy, p. 11; Copyright Michael Cummings/Getty Images, p. 12; Katsuhiro Kojima/Getty Images, p. 13; Jurgen & Christine Sohns/Getty Images, p. 14; Frank Fichtmüller/Getty Images, p. 15; Peter Ivanyi/Shutterstock, p. 16; WILDLIFE GmbH/Alamy, p. 17; James_Lindsay/Shutterstock, p. 18; Arturo de Frias photography/Getty Images, p. 20; Mint Images/Getty Images, p. 22; Biborik/Shutterstock, p. 23.; Naturfoto Honal/Getty Images, p. 26; Paul Tessier/Shutterstock, p. 27; Jupiterimages/Getty Images, p. 28; Eastcott Momatiuk/Getty Images, p. 29. Design elements: iunewind/Shutterstock; Milano M/Shutterstock; Cassel/Shutterstock; Textures and backgrounds/Shutterstock; Print Net/Shutterstock; Ukrainian studio/Shutterstock.

Cover: PHOTO 24/Getty Images; Moelyn Photos/Getty Images.